The Be[st]
New House

Mr. and Mrs. Barnaby
had a lot of grandchildren.
They liked the grandchildren
to come and visit.

The children loved to play
outside on the swing.

They loved to play
inside with the toys.

5

They loved to play
on the computer.

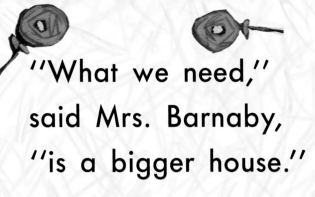

"What we need,"
said Mrs. Barnaby,
"is a bigger house."

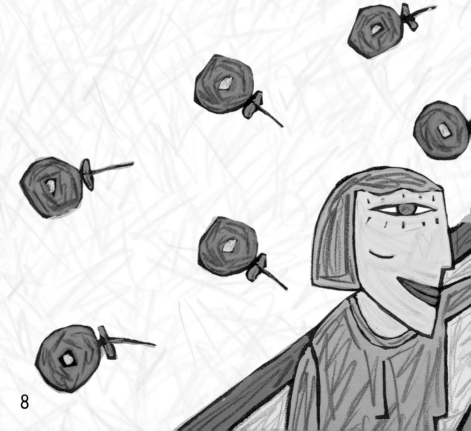

Mr. Barnaby drew a plan.
He added on two new bedrooms.

Buzzzz. Buzzzzz. Buzzzzzz.
Mr. Barnaby's plan came out
of the printer.

"Perfect," said Mrs. Barnaby,
and off she went to town.
She bought wood and nails,
some paint and glue,
and brand new beds.

Together, they made
their little house bigger.

13

The grandchildren came to stay.
They played in the garden.
They played with the toys.
They played on the computer.

They stayed for the night.
There was plenty of room
for everyone.